SOME DISTINCTIONS OF THE CHRISTIAN LIFE

Timothy Cross B.D., ThD., Litt.D

SOME DISTINCTIONS OF THE CHRISTIAN LIFE
Copyright © 2021 by Timothy Cross

ISBN 978-1-8382191-6-1

All rights reserved.
No part of this publication may be reproduced, stored in a retrieval system, or transmitted in any form or by any means, electronic, mechanical, photocopying or otherwise, without prior written consent of the publisher except as provided by under United Kingdom copyright law. Short extracts may be used for review purposes with credits given.

Scripture quotations are from the Revised Standard Version of the Bible, copyright © 1946, 1952, and 1971 the Division of Christian Education of the National Council of the Churches of Christ in the United States of America. Used by permission. All rights reserved.

Published by
Maurice Wylie Media
Your Inspirational Christian Publisher

Publishers' statement: Throughout this book the love for our God is such that whenever we refer to Him, we honour with Capitals. On the other hand, when referring to the devil, we refuse to acknowledge him with any honour to the point of violating grammatical rule and withholding capitalisation.

For more information visit
www.MauriceWylieMedia.com

Contents		Page
Introduction		7
Chapter One:	A Christian rejoices in Christ	9
Chapter Two:	A Christian loves the Bible	14
Chapter Three:	A Christian prays	20
Chapter Four:	A Christian believes in God's providence	27
Chapter Five:	A Christian rejoices in the grace of God	33
Chapter Six:	A Christian lives a particular lifestyle	39
Chapter Seven:	A Christian keeps Sunday special	44
Chapter Eight:	Christians are distinguished by their speech	50
Chapter Nine:	A Christian practises sexual purity	56
Chapter Ten:	A Christian abstains from artificial stimulants	63
Chapter Eleven:	Eternity will finally distinguish Christians from non-Christians	68

Introduction

Outwardly, there would not seem to be much difference between Christians and their non Christian neighbours. Both eat and sleep. Both get married, work, and raise a family. Both have good days and bad days, encouragements and discouragements, good health and bad. But things are not always what they seem. Christians are special people. In 1 Peter 2:9 they are described as 'a chosen race, a royal priesthood, a holy nation, God's own people.'

Truth be told, Christians live their lives on a different plane from others, for Christians are actually the recipients of the saving grace of the triune God, having been 'chosen and destined by God the Father and sanctified by the Spirit for obedience to Jesus Christ and for sprinkling with His blood' (1 Peter 1:2).

It is this intervention of divine grace in the life of a Christian which has made an eternity of difference, and permeates every facet of their existence, not just those aspects which would be considered specifically 'religious.' The Christian Faith is not a religion but a relationship. Christians have come into a relationship with God through Christ. Does this make any difference? It does indeed. It makes an enormous, life-changing difference. We will explore some of these differences in the following pages now when we consider *Some Distinctions of the Christian Life*.

I commit this work to the living God, with the prayer that it will enable and motivate Christians to live more distinctly 'Christianly', and also provide enlightenment for non-Christians, enabling them to know just what a Christian is, what they believe, and why they do and don't do what they do. And if the following chapters should motivate non Christians to seek Christ, my labours will have been rewarded a thousand fold.

Timothy Cross

CHAPTER ONE
A Christian Rejoices in Christ

The word 'Christian' means 'Christ's one.' A Christian would claim to belong to Jesus. Christians are distinguished from their non Christian neighbours by the fact that they have come into a personal relationship with the Lord Jesus Christ. At the heart of the Christian Faith there lies a Person – the incomparable Person of the Lord Jesus Christ. Christianity is Christ. Christ is the gospel and the gospel is Christ. Christians know and rejoice in the saving benefits which only Christ can bestow and only the gospel of Christ can bring. A Christian is one who has been eternally saved by Jesus and expresses gratitude and praise to Him for this, and will do so for all eternity.

Christ is all

In Philippians 3:8 the apostle Paul testified 'I count everything as loss because of the surpassing worth of knowing Christ Jesus my Lord.' Every Christian can echo these words. For a Christian, Christ is everything. He dwarfs all the good things of this life. He makes all our achievements seem relatively puny. He puts all the trials and set backs of life in this world into perspective. For the Christian, Christ is all. His worth surpasses everything.

The apostle Paul, humanly, had much to boast about. He enumerated some of this in Philippians 3. He was born into a Jewish family and thus belonged to the chosen race of God's Old Testament people. He had a privileged upbringing in his faith. As he got older, he took on this faith full board, being meticulous in his attempts to keep the law of God to the letter. Outwardly he appeared to be blameless. Here was an exceedingly zealous man in doing what he believed to be the will of God and gloried in his pedigree and achievements. When it came to Judaism, he was a zealot of zealots! But then He had a life-transforming encounter with the risen, glorified Christ. And after this he considered everything else as 'refuse' (Philippians 3:8). The Greek word for this is 'skubala.' Skubala is not a pleasant or a polite word. It refers to the unpleasant substance you would want to wipe off your shoes should you ever step in it. Paul was using hyperbole. He was expressing his surpassing joy and wonder at knowing the Lord Jesus as his Saviour, Friend and ticket to eternal life and everlasting bliss. And this joy, wonder and delight in Jesus is that which separates the Christian from the non Christian. The driving force in a Christian's life is Christ. The overall ambition of all Christians, having tasted of Christ's salvation is, paradoxically to 'know Him' (Philippians 3:10) – to 'press on to know the LORD' (Hosea 6:3):

> More about Jesus would I know
> More of His grace to others show
> More of His saving fullness see
> More of His love who died for me
>
> More about Jesus let me learn
> More of His holy will discern
> Spirit of God my teacher be
> Showing the things of Christ to me.

Christ's Ones

Acts 11:26 records that *'in Antioch the disciples were for the first time called Christians.'* The term might have originally been a nickname, but it was a good one. They considered themselves as 'Christ's ones.' A Christian is one who belongs to Christ. A Christian is one who has known the saving intervention of Christ in their life, and can thus say personally that 'Christ Jesus has made me His own' (Philippians 3:12). Christians are those who depend on Christ for their eternal salvation, and are trusting Him as their own, personal Saviour, rather than relying on who they are or what they have done, do, or hope to do. Of course, Christ does not come into the frame of reference of a non Christian. Why not? Because, truth be told, the Holy Spirit alone can convince us of our need of Christ and Christ's all-sufficiency for our need.

Knowing Christ as Saviour

Knowing Christ is our Saviour is and forever will be the chief delight of a Christian. A Saviour refers to a rescuer or deliverer. A rescuer or deliverer from what? From the punishment we deserve for our sins; from the liability we owe to God for breaking His law. The very name 'Jesus' means 'Saviour.' A Saviour from what? A Saviour from the wrath of God; a Saviour from eternal hell. It is this which constitutes the Christian gospel – the gospel of Christ. *'You shall call His name Jesus for He will save His people from their sins'* (Matthew 1:21). *'The saying is sure and worthy of full acceptance, that Christ Jesus came into the world to save sinners'* (1 Timothy 1:15). *'The Son of man came to seek and to save the lost'* (Luke 19:10).

How though has Christ saved us from our sins? By paying the penalty for them – by actually taking them upon Himself, when He died on the cross of Calvary. 1 Peter 2:24 says *'He Himself bore our sins in His body on the tree'*. Hebrews 9:28 tells of *'Christ, having been offered once to bear the sins of many'*, and 2 Corinthians 5:21 actually says *'For our sake He made Him to be sin who knew no sin so that in Him we might become the righteousness of God.'*

The gospel of Christ affirms **G**od's **O**wn **S**on **P**aid **E**very Liability. Thus the Christian – one who is trusting in Christ – can rejoice and sing

> My sin, O the bliss of this glorious thought
> My sin not in part but the whole
> Is nailed to the cross, and I bear it no more
> Praise the Lord, praise the Lord, O my soul.

Saving faith in Christ

So a Christian is separated from a non Christian by a personal relationship with the Lord Jesus Christ. A Christian has come to know Christ and His saving benefits. A non Christian sees no need of Christ and has no interest in Him – though their need of Him is absolutely desperate and damnable. A Christian though has been wakened up by the Holy Spirit of God, convicted of their sin and drawn to the foot of the cross and enabled to trust Christ as their own personal Saviour. A Christian is distinguished particularly by saving faith in the Lord Jesus Christ- a faith whereby we have escaped from God's wrath and curse due to us for our sin. What are we talking about here? Let the *Shorter Catechism* explain:

What is faith in Jesus Christ?

Faith in Jesus Christ is a saving grace, whereby we receive and rest upon Him alone for salvation, as He is offered to us in the gospel.

Lawson comments 'Grace means undeserved favour or kindness. A saving grace means an act of God's favour ending in salvation. Faith is such a grace. And it is here said to consist in receiving Christ – that is, in believing what is said of Him in the Bible; and resting upon Him – that is, trusting our souls to Him as our Saviour. We rest on Him alone, and not in anything we may or can do. Our plea is, Christ only.'

A Christian's chief joy therefore is Christ. Sola Christus is the Christian's motto. Christ is and will be proved to be the all sufficient Saviour for our deepest need. The Christian life is thus a Christ-centred life. He is the object of our faith. He is the theme of our praise. He is the source of our joy. His presence in our lives has made an eternity of difference.

> My song shall be of Jesus
> His mercy crowns my days
> He fills my cup with blessings
> And tunes my heart to praise
> My song shall be of Jesus
> The precious Lamb of God
> Who gave Himself my ransom
> And bought me with His blood.

CHAPTER TWO

A Christian Loves the Bible

Christians are distinguished from their non Christian neighbours by a love for and a preoccupation with the Bible. A normal Christian will read the Bible every day and attend a church where the contents of the Bible are believed, explained, applied and proclaimed. The normal Christian life sees a priority given to the Bible, and has a lifetime ambition to both master its contents and be mastered by its contents. A Christian therefore carves out time each day to read the Bible. The Christian life is both formed and transformed by the Bible. A love for the Lord Jesus and a love for the Book which reveals Him go hand in hand. Jesus, the incarnate Word of God, and the Bible, the inspired Word of God are inextricable in Christian experience.

But why are Christians so occupied and preoccupied with the Bible?

The Message of Salvation

A Christian loves the Bible for the Bible alone reveals to us the way of salvation. The Bible reveals the way of salvation to us because the Bible reveals Christ to us, in Whom alone salvation is found. In John 5:39 we read Jesus saying *'You search the scriptures, because you think that in them you have eternal life; and it is they that bear witness to me'*. The over-riding message of the Bible is the message of salvation

– God's salvation of His people through His promised Messiah. The well-known verse of John 3:16 has been well described as 'the Bible within the Bible.' John 3:16 is 'the gospel in a nutshell' when it states *'God so loved the world that He gave His only Son, that whoever believes in Him should not perish but have eternal life.'* Christians have believed in Jesus, and so know the joy of eternal life. But they want to know more! They find this 'more' in the Bible – *'the sacred writings which are able to instruct you for salvation through faith in Jesus Christ'* (2 Timothy 3:15).

The Word of God

A Christian is occupied with the Bible because the Bible is like no other book. It claims to be – and has been proved to be – the very Word of God Himself. It therefore demands and requires our attention like nothing else. 2 Timothy 3:16 tells us that *'All Scripture is inspired by God…'* That is, Holy Scripture is divinely inspired – breathed out by God's Holy Spirit. The Holy Spirit so guided the minds and the pens of the human authors that they wrote exactly what the Divine Author wanted us to know. *'No prophecy ever came by the impulse of man, but men moved by the Holy Spirit spoke from God'* (2 Peter 1:2)1. It is the divine inspiration of the Bible which gives it is unsurpassed authority and ensures it is without error, that is, inerrant. The Bible is the voice of Him Who sits upon the throne! It is the Word of God. It is the Book of God and hence the God of all books – beyond compare, in a category all of its own.

> How precious is the Book divine
> By inspiration given
> Bright as a lamp its doctrines shine
> To guide our way to heaven.

Light in the Darkness

A Christian reads the Bible because a Christian needs the Bible, for guidance is always needed to navigate life's maze. Through reading the Bible we receive enlightenment – divine guidance. *'Thy word is a lamp to my feet and a light to my path'* (Psalm 119:105). The Bible contains God our Maker's instructions; hence it contains the secret of a happy life, a happy death and a happy eternity. 2 Timothy 3:16-17 states *'All Scripture is inspired by God and profitable for teaching* (what is right), *for reproof* (what is not right), *for correction* (for getting right) *and for training in righteousness* (for staying right), *that the man of God may be complete, equipped for every good work.'*

Firm Foundations

The foundation for the Christian life and living thus rests four square on the rock of Holy Scripture. Scripture is the Christian's final authority, for what Scripture says, God Himself says. It is by design that the *Shorter Catechism* which encapsulates the Faith of the Bible begins so:

What is the chief end of man? Man's chief end is to glorify God and to enjoy Him for ever

What rule hath God given to direct us how we may glorify and enjoy Him? The Word of God, which is contained in the Scriptures of the Old and New Testaments, is the only rule to direct us how we may glorify and enjoy Him

What do the Scriptures principally teach? The Scriptures principally teach what man is to believe concerning God and what duty God requires of man.

Lawson's comment on the last quote is apt:

In order to attain the chief end of our life (fellowship with God) the two things most important for us to know are: What we are to believe and What we are to do. These two things the Bible explains to us very fully. It tells us what God is and has done for us, and also what He requires us to do, in order that it may be well with us now and hereafter.

Food for the Soul

A Christian loves the Bible because in the Bible we find spiritual food to sustain our Christian life. Appetite is a sign of life. Food is necessary for life. Dead people don't eat! A Christian has been born again. A Christian has come to eternal life in Christ. This life is to be nurtured, grown and sustained. It is so by the Word of God. A desire to read the Bible thus distinguishes one who has been born again from one who is spiritually dead. In 1 Peter 2:2-3 Peter writes to believers *'Like new born babes, long for the pure spiritual milk that by it you may grow up to salvation; for you have tasted the kindness of the Lord.'* A Christian thus needs the Bible for spiritual sustenance, and the Bible is this necessary food for the soul, prepared and provided for us by Almighty God Himself. *'Thy words were found, and I ate them, and Thy words became to me a joy and the delight of my heart; for I am called by Thy name, O LORD, God of hosts'* (Jeremiah 15:16). *'How sweet are Thy words to my taste, sweeter than honey to my mouth'* (Psalm 119:103).

So a Christian is distinguished from his or her non Christian friends by a love for the Bible. There is no book to compare with it. It is the Book which has given us life. It is the Book which sustains our Christian life. It is a Book which draws us closer to Jesus. John's 'give away' verse explaining why he wrote his Gospel could also be applied equally to all the other sixty five books of the Bible. *'These are written that you may believe that Jesus is the Christ, the Son of God, and that believing you may have life in His name'* (John 20:31).

An anonymous author once wrote the following – words which encapsulate something of the uniqueness and incomparability of the Bible, the Book of God:

This Book contains the mind of God, the state of man, the way of salvation, the doom of sinners and the happiness of believers. Its doctrines are holy, its precepts binding, its histories are true and its decisions are immutable. Read it to be wise, believe it to be safe and practice it to be holy. It contains light to direct you, food to support you and comfort to cheer you. It is the traveller's map, the pilgrim's staff, the pilot's compass, the soldier's sword and the Christian's charter. Here is paradise restored, heaven opened and the gates of hell disclosed. Christ is its grand object, our good its design and the glory of God its end. It should fill the memory, rule the heart and guide the feet. It is a mine of wealth, a paradise of glory and a river of pleasure. It is given you in life, will be opened in judgment, and will be remembered forever. It involves the highest responsibilities, will reward the greatest labours and will condemn all who trifle with its sacred contents.

Truly, there is no book like the Bible!

Holy Bible, Book divine
Precious treasure, thou art mine
Mine to tell me whence I came
Mine to tell me what I am

Mine to chide me when I rove
Mine to show a Saviour's love
Mine thou art to guide and guard
Mine to punish or reward

Mine to comfort in distress
Suffering in this wilderness
Mine to show by living faith
Man can triumph over death

Mine to tell of joys to come
And the rebel sinner's doom
Holy Bible, Book divine
Precious treasure, thou art mine!

CHAPTER THREE
A Christian Prays

Habitual prayer to God is another characteristic of Christians which distinguishes them from their non-Christian neighbours. Not long after his life-changing encounter with the glorified Christ, it was said of Saul of Tarsus *'behold, he is praying'* (Acts 9:11). Prayer is a sign of spiritual life. Just as a healthy, new-born baby cries, likewise, spiritually, when we have been born again, we will and are able to pray to God.

All Christians ensure that they carve out time from their daily schedules to be alone with God and commune with Him in prayer. We have seen that, in the Bible, God speaks to us. In prayer, we reciprocate, for in prayer we speak to God. According to Jesus the secret of prayer is prayer in secret. He said *'When you pray, go into your room and shut the door and pray to your Father who is in secret; and your Father who sees in secret will reward you'* (Matthew 6:6). Christians have every incentive to engage in prayer. Jesus Himself exhorted and still exhorts His followers with the words *'Ask, and it will be given you; seek, and you will find; knock and it will be opened to you. For every one who asks receives, and he who seeks finds, and to him who knocks it will be opened.'* In Psalm 50:15 God Himself says *'Call upon Me in the day of trouble; I will deliver you, and you shall glorify me.'* The God of the Bible is a God who hears and answers the prayers of His children.

A Christian's highest privilege

Prayer is one of the Christian's highest privileges. Prayer is both a Christian's duty and delight. At its simplest, prayer refers to talking to God. The wonder of wonders is that anyone could ever have the ear of the Almighty, the highest Authority of all, but the Bible tells us that Christians do. Ephesians 2:18 tells us that *'through Him* (Christ) *we both have access in one Spirit to the Father.'* Christ's atoning death has reconciled us to God. *'But now, in Christ Jesus, you who once were far off have been brought near in the blood of Christ.'* Thus, through Christ, we may *'with confidence draw near to the throne of grace, that we may receive mercy and find grace to help in time of need'* (Hebrews 4:16). It is through the merits and mediation of Christ alone that the glorious avenue of prayer is opened.

> Behold the throne of grace
> The promise calls us near
> There Jesus shows a smiling face
> And waits to answer prayer
>
> That rich atoning blood
> Which sprinkled round I see
> Provides for those who come to God
> An all-prevailing plea.

What is prayer?

What exactly though is a Christian doing when he or she prays? What is prayer? One of the best definitions is the one given in the *Shorter Catechism* when it states:

Prayer is an offering up of our desires unto God, for things agreeable to His will, in the name of Christ, with confession of our sins and thankful acknowledgement of His mercies.

Lawson comments on this as follows:
Prayer means *asking* of God; and we are here told the following things respecting it: 1. As to its *form* it should be offered to God in the name of Christ; 2. As to its *substance*, it should be for things agreeable to God's will; 3. As to its *manner*, it should be made with humble acknowledgement of our sins, and grateful acknowledgement of God's mercy.

Prayer has various facets to it. It is a many sided diamond. It is helpful to consider some of these facets under the acronym ACTS. This stands for Adoration, Confession, Thanksgiving and Supplication.

Adoration

Praising and adoring God is the highest activity in which any human being can engage. Adoring the majesty of God for who He is lifts us out of ourselves. Reminding ourselves of His greatness and goodness always puts our temporal needs into perspective and acts as a tonic to the soul. There is none greater than God. There is none more worthy of praise. He alone is to be worshipped. Worshipping anyone or anything else actually is idolatry. God alone is God! He is the greatest and most glorious being of all.

God is a Spirit, infinite, eternal and unchangeable in His being, wisdom, power, holiness, justice, goodness and truth (*Shorter Catechism*).

'Great is the LORD, and greatly to be praised, and His greatness is unsearchable' (Psalm 145:3). To adore God is to *'Glory in His holy name'* (Psalm 105:3). It is to respond to the revelation He has given to us of His glory and grace in His Word, and say *'Bless the LORD, O my soul; and all that is within me, bless His holy name! Bless the LORD, O my soul, and forget not all His benefits'* (Psalm 103:1-2).

Christians have reason to praise and adore God. We are the recipients of His grace and mercy. Sinners though we are, we are the objects of His love. He sent His own Son to save us! He took the initiative for our salvation. *'We love because He first loved us'* (1 John 4:19). *'In this the love of God was made manifest among us, that God sent His only Son into the world, so that we might live through Him. In this is love, not that we loved God but that He loved us and sent His Son to be the propitiation for our sins'* (1 John 4:9-10).

Confession

Christians have been adopted into God's family, never to be cast out. Our status and security is eternally secure. Yet our conscious enjoyment of God's fellowship varies and wavers. It can be spoiled by our continuing sin. Paradoxically, although we are righteous in God's sight because of Christ, we are still sinners and continue to sin. *'If we say we have no sin, we deceive ourselves and the truth is not in us'* (1 John 1:8). What is the remedy for this malady? Honest confession to God. *'If we confess our sins, He is faithful and just, and will forgive our sins and cleanse us from all unrighteousness'* (1 John 1:9). This takes humility, but the liberation experienced when we do is better experienced than described. The God and Father of our Lord Jesus Christ is a forgiving God. Praise His name, there is restorative grace with Him. *'As far as the east is from the west, so far does He remove our transgressions from us'* (Psalm 103:12). Proverbs 28:13 tells us *'He who conceals his transgressions will not prosper, but he who confesses and forsakes them will obtain mercy.'*

Thanksgiving

Thanksgiving refers to the verbal articulation of gratitude to God for the blessings He bestows on us:

> Count your many blessings
> Name them one by one
> And it will surprise you
> What the Lord your God has done.

Thanksgiving refers to a verbal appreciation to God for His goodness to us. We thus give thanks to God for both His earthly and eternal blessings – blessings which are physical and blessings which are spiritual. The air we breathe, the food we eat, the clothes we wear, the homes in which we live, the friends we have etc etc... are all ultimately gifts of God. *'Every good endowment and every perfect gift is from above, coming down from the Father of lights with whom there is no variation or shadow due to change'* (James 1:17).

Earthly blessings are enjoyed by all, whether Christian or non-Christian. Yet only Christians give thanks to the Giver. Eternal blessings however are known uniquely to Christians alone. We are referring here to *'the unsearchable riches of Christ'* (Ephesians 3:8) – the 'solid joys and lasting treasures which none but Zion's children know.' A meditation on the grace of God in Christ to us always fills our hearts with gratitude. *'The free gift of God is eternal life in Christ Jesus our Lord'* (Romans 6:23). *'Thanks be to God for His inexpressible gift'* (2 Corinthians 9:15). Thanksgiving to God is thus always a major segment of Christian prayer, and will be for all eternity. *'O give thanks to the LORD, for He is good, for His steadfast love endures for ever'* (Psalm 136:1).

Lastly, we come to:

Supplication

Supplication is related to the word 'supply.' When we 'supplicate' God it is because we or others have an unmet need, and we bring that need to Him, confident that He is able and willing to meet that need. It is a simple case of asking and receiving. It has been well said that prayer is not a matter of overcoming God's reluctance, but taking hold of His willingness.

When it comes to supplication, the Lord Jesus gave an illustration by means of an argument from the lesser to the greater. He said *'What man of you, if his son asks him for bread, will give him a stone? Or if he asks for a fish, will give him a serpent? If you then, who are evil, know how to give good gifts to your children, how much more will your Father who is in heaven give good things to those who ask Him!'* (Matthew 7:9-11).

Asking, therefore, is one of the laws of the kingdom of heaven. *'You do not have, because you do not ask'* (James 4:2). *'My God will supply every need of yours according to His riches in glory in Christ Jesus'* (Philippians 4:19).

The elements of prayer

There then we have the basic elements of Christian prayer – made possible through the merits and mediation of the Lord Jesus and assisted by the help of the Holy Spirit who is promised to all of God's children. *'The Spirit helps us in our weakness; for we do not know how to pray as we ought, but the Spirit Himself intercedes for us with sighs too deep for words'* (Romans 8:26). The elements of prayer? Think of ACTS. Adoration. Confession. Thanksgiving. Supplication.

The habitual practice of prayer, as we have already intimated, is that which separates the Christian from the non-Christian. Christians alone are privy to this immense privilege, not because they are better or more talented than their non Christian neighbours, but solely because of the grace of God in Christ. *'We have confidence to enter the sanctuary* (that is, the very presence of God) *by the blood of Jesus, by the new and living way which He opened for us through the curtain, that is, through His flesh'* (Hebrews 10:19-20).

In Philippians 4:6 Paul writes *'Have no anxiety about anything, but in everything by prayer and supplication with thanksgiving, let your requests be made known to God.'* 1 Peter 5:7 exhorts *'Cast all your anxieties on Him for He cares about you.'* Truly, 'O what peace we often forfeit, O what needless pain we bear, all because we do not carry, everything to God in prayer.' When we realise the wonder of prayer, it is very strange that we Christians do not exploit this means of grace and channel of blessing more than we do.

>Come my soul, thy suit prepare
>Jesus loves to answer prayer
>He Himself has bid thee pray
>Therefore will not say thee nay
>
>Thou art coming to a King
>Large petitions with thee bring
>For His grace and power are such
>None can ever ask too much.

CHAPTER FOUR

A Christian Believes in Divine Providence

The events and happenings in our lives are many and various. At times they seem chaotic. We can't say that we have control over much that comes our way. We have good days and bad days. We have encouragements and disappointments. We might find ourselves currently married or single, healthy or sick, employed or redundant ... We make our plans, and these might be fulfilled or completely dashed. How do you make sense of all this? The non Christian would say that it is all down to 'good fortune' when things go well, or it is down to 'bad luck' when things go the other way. It is all down to 'chance.' A Christian however sees the hand of God behind all the events in his or her life, large and small, good and bad. Why? Because the Bible teaches that Almighty God is in absolute control of all things generally and the lives of His children particularly. He sovereignly superintends all things. He is totally sovereign and He is the one behind all secondary causes. *'For from Him and through Him and to Him are <u>all things</u>'* (Romans 11:36). *'The LORD has established His throne in the heavens, and His kingdom rules <u>over all</u>'* (Psalm 103:19).

The Providence of God

The shorthand for the above is to say that a Christian believes in and takes great comfort from divine providence. But what is divine providence? Divine providence is a facet of God's very God-ness. He has His eternal plan, and He is working out all things in accordance with that eternal plan. God's providence is the execution of His eternal decree. What He has pre-determined in eternity past, He will most surely bring about in time. He is almighty God, and nothing can hinder, thwart or frustrate Him from doing what He wills. The *Shorter Catechism* states:

The decrees of God are His eternal purpose, according to the counsel of His will, whereby, for His own glory, He hath foreordained whatsoever comes to pass.

God executeth His decrees in the works of creation and providence.

God's works of providence are His most holy, wise and powerful preserving and governing all His creatures and all their actions.

Christians take their cue from the Lord Jesus Christ, and the Lord Jesus most certainly believed in divine providence. He Himself came to earth to execute God's eternal plan of salvation by dying in the place of God's chosen people to procure their eternal salvation. The cross was no accident but an appointment. In Matthew 10:29 He teaches that God's providence extends even to seemingly insignificant details. There He says *'Are not two sparrows sold for a penny? And not one of them will fall to the ground without your Father's will.'* He said this for the encouragement of God's children. He was arguing from the lesser to the greater. If God's providential eye extends even to sparrows, how much more so does it extend to those made in His image and redeemed by the blood of His Son? So Jesus went on to say *'But even the hairs of your head are all numbered (by God). Fear not, therefore; you are of more value than many sparrows'* (Matthew 10:30-31).

Let us now see some of the details as to what the Bible teaches about divine providence.

Our first birth and the days of our lives

Scripture teaches that both the day of our birth and the day our are death are not accidental but providential. The omniscient God could thus say to Jeremiah *'Before I formed you in the womb I knew you, and before you were born I consecrated you ...'* (Jeremiah 1:5). We had no say in the time or place of our birth. God did! – *'having determined allotted periods and the boundaries of their habitation'* (Acts 17:26). It is *'In Him we live and move and have our being'* (Acts 17:28). We are actually immortal until God's purposes for us on earth are fulfilled. We will not die too soon, or breathe a moment longer than God has predestined. *For 'In Thy book were written, every one of them, the days that were formed for me, when as yet there was none of them'* (Psalm 139:16).

Our second birth

Scripture teaches that the date and time of our new birth are not accidental but providential. *'those whom He predestined He also called; and those whom He called He also justified'* (Romans 8:30). Christians are actually Christians, not so much because they chose to be but because God Himself chose them to be. *'He chose us in Him before the foundation of the world ...'* (Ephesians 1:4). Thus, those chosen by God in eternity past, will most certainly hear the call of God in time. The Holy Spirit will regenerate them – bestow on them the new birth. They will be drawn to Christ and enabled to put their faith in Him for their eternal salvation. Redemption is divine – both divinely ordained, divinely accomplished and divinely applied.

God's providence then is all-embracing. It embraces the believer's first and second births. It embraces the day of our birth and the day of our death. It embraces all the days in-between:

> Sovereign Ruler of the skies
> Ever gracious, ever wise!
> All my times are in Thy hand
> All events at Thy command
>
> His decree, who formed the earth
> Fixed my first and second birth
> Parents, native place and time
> All appointed were by Him
>
> He that formed me in the womb
> He shall guide me to the tomb
> All my times shall ever be
> Ordered by His wise decree.

This last stanza reminds us that Scripture teaches that all the events and circumstances of our earthly lives are not accidental but providential.

The events of our lives

God's will, will be done! He is almighty God. His purposes of grace and glory will be achieved both for His world and for our individual lives. After undergoing much suffering, Job was forced to bow before God and confess *'I know that Thou canst do all things, and that no purpose of Thine can be thwarted'* (Job 42:2). In Philippians 1:6 we are assured that *'He who began a good work in you will bring it to completion at the day of Jesus Christ.'* Then famously, in Romans 8:28 we read that God is actually working all the events of our lives for our ultimate blessing. *'We know that in everything God works for good with those who love Him, who are called according to His purpose.'* Does this 'everything' include our losses and crosses, the disappointments, the stresses and strains, the difficulties and devastations, and all that pains and perplexes us ...? The 'good' that seemed to be denied us and the 'bad' which we never asked for? Yes. The *'everything'* in Romans 8:28 means what it says and says what it means. God is all loving and all wise. He knows what He is doing in our lives, even when we don't. Cowper was wise when he wrote:

> Judge not the Lord by feeble sense
> But trust Him for His grace
> Behind a frowning providence
> He hides a smiling face.

Knowing what we know of the God revealed in the Bible, when we cannot understand His hand in our lives, we can surely trust His heart. 'Faith believes, nor questions how.' God knows what is best for us!

A Christian is thus distinguished from a non-Christian by a steadfast belief in divine providence, through all the ups and downs and highs and lows of this earthly life. God is good, and, as regards His children 'in everything works for good.' Here is the only true anchor for the soul.

In summary, the *Heidelberg Catechism* says this:

Q. What do you understand by the providence of God?

A. The almighty and everywhere present power of God, whereby, as it were by His hand, He still upholds heaven and earth, with all creatures; and so governs them, that herbs and grass, rain and drought, fruitful and barren years, meat and drink, health and sickness, riches and poverty and yea, all things, come not by chance, but by His fatherly hand.

Q. What does it profit us to know that God has created, and by His providence still upholds all things?

A. That we may be patient in adversity; thankful in prosperity; and for what is future, have good confidence in our faithful God and Father, that no creature shall separate us from His love; since all creatures are so in His hand, that without His will they cannot so much as move.

> Great providence of heaven
> What wonders shine
> In its profound display
> Of God's design
> It guards the dust of earth
> Commands the hosts above
> Fulfils the mighty plan
> Of His great love.

CHAPTER FIVE

A Christian Rejoices in the Grace of God

Every Christian can concur with Paul's words in 1 Corinthians 15:10 when he testified *'By the grace of God I am what I am.'* Even the finest Christian on earth will never graduate beyond the words of the following hymn and testimony:

> Naught have I gotten but what I received
> Grace hath bestowed it since I have believed
> Boasting excluded, pride I abase
> I'm only a sinner saved by grace!
>
> Only a sinner saved by grace!
> Only a sinner saved by grace!
> This is my story – to God be the glory –
> I'm only a sinner saved by grace.

A Christian is distinguished from a non-Christian by an awareness of and a constant marvelling in the grace of God and the God of grace. God's grace refers to the love which He pours out on the undeserving and the ill-deserving. The root cause of a Christian's salvation lies not in themselves, but in the grace of God and the God of grace. Perhaps the most famous Christian hymn which celebrates salvation by divine grace is the one written by John Newton:

> Amazing grace, how sweet the sound
> That saved a wretch like me
> I once was lost but now am found
> Was blind but now I see.

Human merit

It is in the realm of grace that the Christian world view is infinitely and radically different from the non Christian one. Grace does not come into this world's frame of reference. The evolution emanating from Darwinism which has permeated many areas of society, for instance, teaches 'the survival of the fittest.' The world of work is built on human merit – rewards for good work and threats if standards are not met. In the human 'rat race' wages are earned by graft. Targets have to be met. Only the best reach the top of the career ladder – the most highly qualified, the most experienced, the one who has proved his or her worth etc. The world of work knows nothing of grace. It is a 'meritocracy.'

In non-Christian religions and sub-Christian religion human merit also figures highly. Popular myth considers that heaven is gained by merit – by 'good deeds.' On the Day of Judgment God will supposedly weigh up our 'good deeds' and our 'bad deeds.' If the good deeds outweigh the bad ones, the door of heaven is opened. But if our 'bad deeds' outweigh the good ones, the door into heaven is barred, and the gates of hell are opened. All this has no room for divine grace, and all this has no room for the cross of Christ. The heresy has an ancient pedigree. In the first century, Paul felt compelled to write to the churches of Galatia, as the Christians in the province of Galatia were being troubled by some who were peddling a human works based salvation. Hence in Galatians 2:21 Paul wrote *'I do not nullify the grace of God; for if justification* (salvation) *were through the law* (that is, what we do/our meritorious works), *then Christ died to no purpose.'*

Saved by grace alone

In Ephesians 2:8,9 we read the glorious affirmation *'For by grace you have been saved through faith; and this is not your own doing, it is the gift of God – not because of works, lest any man should boast.'* Divine grace is the touchstone and distinguishing mark of biblical Christianity – and divine grace rules out any notion of human merit. According to the Bible, salvation is by divine grace, not human graft – divine mercy not human merit. Salvation was procured by the finished, perfect work of Christ and is not and cannot be achieved by the unfinished, imperfect works of human beings. Truth be told, if salvation is not by God's grace, no one would ever be saved at all. Why? Because we cannot meet God's perfect demands. We are sinners. We are 'in the red' with God because of our sins. We cannot be saved by our merits because we have no merits sufficient to put Almighty God in our debt. We are all in debt to Him because of our sin – who we are and what we do. Unless our sin is dealt with, we will be eternally in debt to Him, and pay the price for this ourselves in a terrible, eternal hell ...

The Divine remedy

What then is the remedy for our damnable human sin? The grace of God – or more specifically, the grace of God in the Lord Jesus Christ. Salvation by grace is another way of saying that salvation is by God. It is a free gift. Romans 3:23-24 *reads 'Since all have sinned and fall short of the glory of God, they are justified* (that is, acquitted) *by His grace as a gift, through the redemption which is in Christ Jesus.'*

Tri-une grace

Christians are Christians therefore, not because of any merit intrinsic to themselves, but because of the grace of the Trin-une God. Scripture reveals that God the Father, in His grace, chose them for salvation before the foundation of the world.

A Christian is a Christian, not because of anything they have done, but because of what God the Father has done in His grace. He sent His Son to pay the penalty for their sins on Calvary's cross. Romans 3:25 tells us that Jesus was the One *'whom God put forward as a propitiation by His blood.'*

Christians are Christians, not because of what they have done, but because of the gracious ministry of the Holy Spirit in their lives. He is the one who convicted us of our sin and need. He is the one who showed us our need of Christ and the Christ for our need. He is the one who drew us to Christ and nurtured in us saving faith in Him, enabling us to avail ourselves of His saving merits.

Salvation therefore is by grace alone – by the grace of the Tri-une God. Peter opens his first letter to some scattered Christians who were going through some terrible times by reminding them of this. Life in this world notwithstanding, they were yet objects of the unmerited favour of the true and living God – *'chosen and destined by God the Father and sanctified by the Spirit for obedience to Jesus Christ and sprinkling with His blood. May grace and peace be multiplied to you'* (1 Peter 1:2).

The touchstone of the true Faith

Salvation by divine grace then is the hallmark of the Christian Faith. The Christian gospel is *'the gospel of the grace of God'* (Acts 20:24). Grace refers to God's unmerited favour and undeserved kindness. In mercy He does not give us what we truly deserve. In grace He bestows on us what we don't deserve. It is a case of everything for nothing to those who don't deserve anything! It is this salvation by the grace of God which distinguishes the Christian Faith from all other faiths. It is a rejoicing in the wonder of God's saving grace which differentiates the Christian from the non Christian, and motivates them to live a life pleasing to God out of gratitude for the divine grace they have received. Yes, our sin condemns us – but God's grace in Christ is greater than our sin! *'For where sin increased, grace abounded all the more, so that as sin reigned in death, grace also might reign through righteousness to eternal life through Jesus Christ or Lord'* (Romans 5:20-21).

Christians are trophies of God's saving grace, and thank God constantly for the triumph of His saving grace in their lives.

> By grace I'm saved, grace free and boundless
> My soul believe and doubt it not
> Why stagger at this word of promise?
> Hath Scripture ever falsehood taught?
> No! Then this word must true remain
> By grace, thou too shalt heaven gain
>
> By grace! None dare lay claim to merit
> Our works and conduct have no worth
> God in His love sent our Redeemer
> Christ Jesus, to this sinful earth
> His death did for our sin atone
> And we are saved by grace alone
>
> By grace! O, mark this word of promise
> When thou art by thy sins oppressed
> When Satan plagues thy troubled conscience
> And when thy heart is seeking rest
> What reason cannot comprehend
> God by His grace to thee doeth send

By grace! This ground of faith is certain
So long as God is true, it stands
What saints have penned by inspiration
What in His Word our God commands
What our whole faith must rest upon
Is grace alone, grace in His Son.
(Christian L. Scheidt 1709-61)

CHAPTER SIX

A Christian Lives a Particular Lifestyle

Motivations

Everyone is driven and motivated by something. It might be a desire for riches, fame, possessions, position, prestige or comfort. Or it might be for something necessary but ordinary, for example, the need to provide for our family.

Christians however are different. The one, overarching desire in them, planted there by God's grace, is the desire to live a life which is pleasing to God – or as pleasing to Him as is humanly possible for a sinner saved by grace. This was Paul's desire. And likewise his prayer for other believers was that they should *'lead a life worthy of the Lord, fully pleasing to Him, bearing fruit in every good work and increasing in the knowledge of God'* (Colossians 1:10).

Motivation is central to our lives. We are driven by what motivates us, and a Christian is motivated to please God. This is so, not to earn His favour, but because we have received His favour. It is not with a view to being saved, but because we have actually already been saved. Salvation is all of divine grace. Works are all done out of gratitude for this wonderful divine grace we have received:

> I cannot work my soul to save
> That work my Lord alone has done
> But I will work like any slave
> For Love of God's dear Son.

Christians then are, and are called to live and be known by a distinctly Christian lifestyle. The Christian life is a life to be lived. Our salvation is a salvation to be worked out day by day. We are saved by faith, not works, yet faith works! Our works and lifestyle will betray our saving faith or lack of it. James said *'For as the body apart from the spirit is dead, so faith apart from works is dead'* (James 2:26).

Saving faith leads to a life of gratitude to God. Salvation is not by works, yet with the help of God, this salvation is to be worked out. Both of these facets are plain when we read Ephesians 2:8-10, where Paul explains *'For by grace you have been saved through faith; and this is not your own doing, it is the gift of God – not because of works, lest any man should boast. For we are His workmanship, created in Christ Jesus for good works, which God prepared beforehand, that we should walk in them.'* Christians are called to be different from their non-Christian neighbours because by the grace of God they are different! To the glory of God, Christians are under the authority of the Word of God. There are some things they do which their non-Christian neighbours do not do, and there are some things they do not do which their non-Christian neighbours do.

In Philippians 2:12-13 Paul encouraged his Christian friends in Philippi to *'work out your own salvation with fear and trembling; for God is at work in you, both to will and to work for His good pleasure.'* He went on to say that this entails being *'blameless and innocent, children of God without blemish in the midst of a crooked and perverse generation, among whom you shine as lights in the world, holding fast the Word of life.'* Here, Paul was echoing some words of his Master, for Jesus likewise said to His followers *'Let your light so shine before men, that they may see your good works and give glory to your Father who is in heaven'* (Matthew 5:16).

Living the life

Those of us who frequent the locker rooms of gyms know what it is to admire those who 'live the life', that is, those who are dedicated to their exercise regime, and are also careful about what they eat, and ensure that they also get enough rest to recover.

In the spiritual realm, Christians too are called to 'live the life.' As we have seen, this entails having a disciplined time of prayer and Bible study each day, but it also touches and permeates our public activity as well as our private times with God. Paul exhorts *'let your manner of life be worthy of the gospel of Christ'* (Philippians 1:27). There is and there can be no area of our life which is not affected and impacted by the gospel. The gospel becomes part of our very fibre and outlook.

Our friends in Ephesus

The six chapters of Paul's letter to the Ephesians have a beautiful symmetry to them. Paul balances doctrine and duty, belief and behaviour, creed and deed. The latter flow from the former. What we believe determines how we behave. In Ephesians 1-3, Paul glories in the doctrine of divine grace. In Ephesians 4-6 he explains that those who have received this divine grace are to be characterised by a lifestyle – attitudes and actions – which reveal that they are indeed the objects of divine grace. Christians are called to stand out! Christians are called to shine for Jesus. *'For once you were darkness, but now you are light in the Lord; walk as children of light'* (Ephesians 5:8*) 'and try to learn what is pleasing to the Lord'* (Ephesians 5:10). Paul therefore begins chapter four with an exhortation to live a Christian lifestyle compatible with being the adopted children of God. *'I therefore, a prisoner for the Lord, beg you to lead a life worthy of the calling to which you have been called'* (Ephesians 4:1), that is *'to lead a life worthy of God, who calls you into His own kingdom and glory'* (1 Thessalonians 1:12). Similarly, Ephesians

5 begins *'Therefore* (that is, in the light of the divine mercy you have received) *be imitators of God, as beloved children. And walk in love, as Christ loved us and gave Himself up for us, a fragrant offering and sacrifice to God'* (Ephesians 5:1-2).

Saints alive!

One of the most common New Testament words to designate a Christian is that of a 'saint.' Paul addresses the church at Corinth as *'those sanctified in Christ Jesus, called to be saints together with all those who in every place call on the name of our Lord Jesus Christ, both their Lord and ours'* (1 Corinthians 1:2). The word 'saint' means 'a set apart one', that is, set apart by God for God. Christians are those who have been set apart by God for God – chosen by God, redeemed by Christ and sanctified by the Holy Spirit. Christian living is therefore the outworking of who we are. We are called to live out our Christian lives in the particular sphere in which God has placed us – family, work, leisure etc. We are in this world but not of this world. Christian living is simply the living out of a life devoted to God. Christian 'being' and Christian living cannot be separated. We *are* Christians. We are thus to *live* as Christians – *'not ... conformed to this world but ... transformed by the renewal of your mind, that you may prove what is the will of God, what is good and acceptable and perfect'* (Romans 12:2). Jesus does not call us out of this fallen world, but He calls us to be His witnesses in this fallen world. He calls us to act as salt and light. Salt prevents decay. Light dispels darkness. This world is rotten and rotting because of sin. This world is lost in the darkness of sin. It is in this fallen world that Jesus calls us to stand out. He says *'You are the salt of the earth'* (Matthew 5:13) and *'You are the light of the world. A city on a hill cannot be hid ...'* (Matthew 5:14).

So Christians, saved by grace, are saved and motivated to live a life pleasing to God. We are and are called to be Christian in behaviour as well as belief. We are to stand out for Jesus. We are to shine for Jesus. We are called to be different from our non Christian neighbours because by God's grace we *are* different from our non Christian neighbours. We belong to Jesus! Belonging to Jesus impinges on every area of our lives. *'So whether you eat or drink, or whatever you do, do all to the glory of God'* (1 Corinthians 10:31).

> Teach me, my God and King,
> in all things thee to see,
> and what I do in anything
> to do it as for thee.
>
> A man that looks on glass,
> on it may stay his eye;
> or if he pleaseth, through it pass,
> and then the heaven espy.
>
> All may of thee partake;
> nothing can be so mean,
> which with this tincture, "for thy sake,"
> will not grow bright and clean.
>
> A servant with this clause
> makes drudgery divine:
> who sweeps a room, as for thy laws,
> makes that and the action fine.
>
> This is the famous stone
> that turneth all to gold;
> for that which God doth touch and own
> cannot for less be told.

CHAPTER SEVEN
A Christian Keeps Sunday Special

Just another day?

Is there anything which distinguishes Sunday, the first day of the week, from the other six days? Apparently not. Here in the UK shops are open on Sundays, and do a very good trade. Large sporting events also occur on Sundays and draw large crowds. People also find Sunday a good day on which to do the jobs they have not had time for during the working week – mowing the lawn, washing the car and maintenance of the house. They may even use the time to watch a boxed set of DVDs, or catch up on television they have missed …

The Christian's special day

The Christian's attitude towards and use of Sundays distinguishes and differentiates them radically from their non Christian friends. For the Christian, Sunday is a special day. It is their Sabbath Day. It is 'The Lord's Day.' God's commandment is clear *'Remember the Sabbath Day to keep it holy'* (Exodus 20:8). The word 'holy' here means 'different, separate, distinct.' It means 'set apart by God for God.' Because of this, Christians keep one day of the week as a day especially devoted to God – to His Word, His ordinances, His church and His worship.

Keeping the Sabbath is both a duty and a delight. Christians 'keep the Sabbath' and find that paradoxically, the Sabbath keeps them. It keeps their eternal perspective; it keeps the fires of devotion burning; it gives spiritual sustenance for living in the secular world on the other six days.

The word 'Sabbath' comes from the Hebrew word to cease or rest. On the Sabbath the Christian ceases from the legitimate, secular concerns of the week and gives greater attention to divine matters, turning from the things of time to the things of eternity, turning from temporal, earthly matters to eternal, heavenly matters. The Christian keeps Sunday special and delights in doing so. There is no day like the Sabbath Day. The Puritans used to refer to it as 'the market day of the soul.'

The priority of divine worship

Central to the Sabbath day is the public worship of Almighty God – gathering with other believers to sing God's praise, hear His Word and know precious fellowship in the things of the redeeming, risen and reigning Christ. Christians can relate to the Psalmist when he wrote *'This is the day which the LORD has made, let us rejoice and be glad in it'* (Psalm 118:24) and *'I was glad when they said to me, 'Let us go to the house of the LORD!''* (Psalm 122:1).

> O Day of rest and gladness
> O Day of joy and light
> O balm of care and sadness
> Most beautiful, most bright!
> On thee the high and lowly
> Through ages joined in tune
> Sing 'Holy, holy, holy'
> To the great God Triune

> On thee at the creation
> The light first had its birth
> On thee, for our salvation
> Christ rose from depths of earth
> On thee our Lord victorious
> The Spirit sent from heaven
> And thus on thee most glorious
> A triple light was given
>
> Today on weary nations
> The heavenly manna falls
> To holy convocations
> The silver trumpet calls
> When gospel light is glowing
> With pure and radiant beams
> And living water flowing
> With soul refreshing streams.

Why the first day?

The fourth commandment – part of the moral law, given by God, binding for all time – reads *'Remember the Sabbath day to keep it holy. Six days you shall labour, and do all your work; but the seventh day is a Sabbath to the LORD your God ...'* (Exodus 20:8-10), Yet Christians observe the first day of the week, not the seventh day, as their Sabbath day. This has been the case for the last two thousand years or so. *'On the first day of the week, when we were gathered together to break bread, Paul talked with them ...'* (Acts 20:7). What accounts for the change in the Sabbath Day from the seventh to the first? Something momentous must have happened to alter a commandment of God ... The momentous event was the resurrection of Christ. Christ conquered the grave and rose from the dead on the first day of the week. It was *'after the Sabbath, toward the dawn of the first day of the week* (that) *Mary Magdalene and the other Mary went to see the sepulchre'* (Matthew 28:1) and there heard the joyful news *'Do not be afraid; for I know that you seek Jesus who was crucified. He is not here; for He has risen, as He said. Come, see the place where He lay'* (Matthew 28:5-6). Ever since then Christians have observed the first day of the week as the Christian Sabbath, and have gathered together to worship their risen Lord and Saviour, Who presences Himself with them by His Holy Spirit when they gather in His name. The Christian Sabbath is thus a weekly reminder of the most attested and epochal fact of history: the resurrection of Christ. Christians wake up on a Sunday morning with an infinitely different spirit and attitude from their non Christian neighbours. They say words to the effect of:

> Again the Lord's own day is here
> The day to Christian people dear
> As week by week it bids them tell
> How Jesus rose from death and hell.

Living in a Christian counter-culture

Sadly, in recent decades, the Lord's Day has become more and more secular and indistinguishable from the other days. But Christians live and are called to live in a Christian counter-culture, different from the ways of the world. Christians are exhorted to guard the Sabbath. When they do, they will find that the Sabbath guards them from much of the world's ways which are contrary to the ways of God. The fourth commandment is still binding. For our blessing and benefit, God commands us to 'Remember the Sabbath Day, to keep it holy.' The day is intended for our good. It is ordained by God for our blessing. If we disregard God's instructions, it will surely be to our own loss and detriment. The *Shorter Catechism* states:

What is required in the fourth commandment?
The fourth commandment requireth the keeping holy to God such set times as He hath appointed in His Word, expressly one whole day in seven, to be a holy Sabbath to Himself.

Which day of the seven hath God appointed to be the weekly Sabbath?
From the beginning of the world to the resurrection of Christ, God appointed the seventh day of the week to be the weekly Sabbath; and the first day of the week ever since, to continue to the end of the world, which is the Christian Sabbath.

How is the Sabbath to be sanctified?
The Sabbath is to be sanctified by a holy resting all that day, even from such worldly employments and recreations as are lawful on other days; and spending the whole time in the public and private exercises of God's worship, except so much as is to be taken up in the works of necessity and mercy.

May God give us grace to *'call the Sabbath a delight and the holy day of the LORD honourable'* (Isaiah 58:13).

> Jesus, we love to meet
> On this Thy holy day
> We worship round Thy seat
> On this Thy holy day
> Thou tender, heavenly Friend
> To Thee our prayers ascend
> O'er all our spirits bend
> On this Thy holy day
>
> We dare not trifle now
> On this Thy holy day
> In silent awe we bow
> On this Thy holy day

Check every wandering thought
And let us all be taught
To serve Thee as we ought

We listen to Thy Word
On this Thy holy day
Bless all that we have heard
On this Thy holy day
Go with us when we part
And to each needy heart
Thy saving grace impart
On this Thy holy day.

CHAPTER EIGHT

Christians are Distinguished by their Speech

To express ourselves through the medium of language and speech is a remarkable and complex facility. Human beings are able to communicate verbally, and here we reflect something of the image of God our Maker, for the God of the Bible is a God who communicates through words. Hebrews 1:1-2 reads *'In many and various ways God spoke of old to our fathers by the prophets, but in these last days He has spoken to us by a Son ...'*

Speech betrays us

Our habitual speech actually reveals something of the state of our hearts – who we really are. It is the fruit of the root. The Lord Jesus said *'Either make the tree good, and its fruit good; or make the tree bad and the fruit bad; for the tree is known by its fruit. You brood of vipers! How can you speak good when you are evil? For out of the abundance of the heart the mouth speaks. The good man out of his good treasure brings forth good, and the evil man out of his evil treasure brings forth evil'* (Mathew 12:33-35).

Christian salvation involves being renewed on the inside by God's Holy Spirit. Salvation is from the inside out! God's promise is *'A new heart I will give you, and a new spirit I will put within you; and I will take out of your flesh the heart of stone and give you a heart of flesh. And I will put my spirit within you and cause you to walk in my statutes and be careful to observe my ordinances'* (Ezekiel 36:26-27).

So every Christian has been given a new heart and nature by God. *'Therefore, if any one is in Christ, he is a new creation ...'* (2 Corinthians 5:17). God enables us to respond to His love and grace in Christ. He gives us His Holy Spirit, enabling us to live in a way which pleases Him. Christian salvation thus permeates every faculty of our being and every area of our lives, and this particularly includes the way we talk and the language we use. Tongues that were once used to blaspheme the Lord are now employed in the praise of the Lord! *'I will bless the LORD at all times; His praise shall continually be in my mouth'* (Psalm 34:1). *'He put a new song in my mouth, a song of praise to our God'* (Psalm 40:3). The Christian's speech therefore reflects the state of the Christian's heart. Romans 10:9: *'If you confess with your lips that Jesus is Lord and believe in your heart that God raised Him from the dead, you will be saved. For man believes with his heart and so is justified, and he confesses with his lips and so is saved.'*

Bad language

Christians are thus distinguished by their speech, and ought to be distinguished by their speech. We live, of course, in an environment where 'bad language', swearing and, sadly, blasphemy are common place. Blasphemy – that is, taking the Lord's name in vain – reveals the spiritual condition of the blasphemer. It shows *'There is no fear of God before their eyes'* (Romans 3:18). Foul language reveals that the one who utters it is unregenerate, and needs to be born anew by God's Spirit.

Romans 3:10 ff. states *'None is righteous, no not one', no one understands, no one seeks for God ... Their throat is an open grave, they use their tongues to deceive. The venom of asps is under their lips. Their mouth is full of curses and bitterness ...'* Here is Paul's diagnosis of unregenerate men and women. Even the way they speak reveals their need of a Saviour. It reveals that they are guilty before God and need to be made right with Him through the Lord Jesus Christ.

Christian language

Christians are called to stand out from the crowd by their speech – by both what they say and by what they do not say. Paul's exhortation to the believers in Ephesus is valid for Christians in all ages: *'Let no evil talk come out of your mouths, but only such as is good for edifying, as fits the occasion, that it may impart grace to those who hear'* (Ephesians 4:29). Then in Colossians 4:5-6 he says *'Conduct yourselves wisely toward outsiders, making the most of the time. Let your speech always be gracious, seasoned with salt, so that you may know how you ought to answer every one.'* Seasoned with salt! It is a picture of speech that is pure and wholesome. God give us grace to speak so. If our speech is the same as a non Christian, we have reason to doubt our salvation, for James says bluntly *'If any one thinks he is religious and does not bridle his tongue but deceives his heart, this man's religion is vain'* (James 1:26).

The Name above all names

The frequent use of blasphemy – using the blessed name of Jesus as a swear word or expletive – in both the media and society in general, is a trend which disturbs all Christians, and rightly so. A true Christian would never take the Saviour's name in vain, and shudders when they hear others doing so. A Christian will always be careful as to how they speak the name of Jesus, and will always speak of Him reverently. This is so for two reasons:

First of all, we owe our eternal salvation to the Lord Jesus Christ. We can say *'the life I now live I live by faith in the Son of God, who loved me and gave Himself for me'* (Galatians 2:20). Christians love the Lord Jesus Christ, albeit imperfectly. We are indebted to His love. We rightly take offence if someone slanders or belittles a member of our own family. We react to such with a reflex reaction. How much more then is this so when someone belittles the very Son of God who has procured our eternal salvation. Christians will always speak well and carefully of the Lord Jesus Christ. His name is infinitely precious to us:

> How sweet the Name of Jesus sounds
> In a believer's ear
> It soothes his sorrows, heals his wounds
> And drives away his fear
>
> Dear Name! The rock on which I build
> My shield and hiding place
> My never-failing treasury filled
> With boundless stores of grace.

Secondly, Christians will always reverence the name of Jesus, and be troubled when others fail to do so, as the commandment of God, binding for all time, requires that we do so.

The third commandment

Disrespecting God's name generally reveals a lack of the fear of God. Disrespecting God's name is a breaking of the third commandment of God, with all the dreadful and damnable consequences which breaking

God's law brings. The third commandment stipulates: *'You shall not take the name of the LORD your God in vain, for the LORD will not hold him guiltless who takes His name in vain'* (Exodus 20:7). What does this third commandment mean, and what are its implications? Let the *Shorter Catechism* explain:

What is required in the third commandment?
The third commandment requireth the holy and reverent use of God's names, titles, attributes, ordinances, Word and works.

What is forbidden in the third commandment?
The third commandment forbiddeth all profaning or abusing of anything whereby God maketh Himself known.

What is the reason annexed to the third commandment?
The reason annexed to the third commandment is, that however the breakers of this commandment may escape punishment from men, yet the LORD our God will not suffer them to escape His righteous judgment.

Lawson's explanatory comment is as follows:

This commandment tells how to treat the Name of God, and by His Name is meant everything by which He is named to us or specially made known. To take God's name in vain is to use it for a vain or frivolous purpose; and we break this command by profane swearing, or by irreverently using God's name. We recognise this command when we pray 'Hallowed be Thy Name.'

So Christians are and are to be distinguished by the way they speak. Salvation – the new birth – permeates every area of our lives, including the employment of the tongue. Of course, no Christian is sinless! We are a work in progress. This being so, God give us grace to control our tongues. We have two ears but only one tongue! James wrote *'Let every man be quick to hear, slow to speak, slow to anger'* (James 1:19). And the Psalmist, knowing the power of the tongue for good or ill prayed *'Set a guard over my mouth, O LORD, keep watch over the door of my lips'* (Psalm 141:3). We might do well to pray the same prayer.

CHAPTER NINE

A Christian Practises Sexual Purity

Here in the 'liberal' West, we live in a highly sexualised environment. We are bombarded with sexuality of all kinds in its heterosexual, homosexual, transsexual and other forms. The prevailing attitudes to both sex and relationships have changed drastically over recent decades. What was once considered a perversion and was illegal by law, is now legal, promoted and even celebrated. Whereas once it was taboo to have a child out of wedlock, now it is quite commonplace and considered normal. Whereas once men who dressed up in women's clothes were objects of mirth and suspicion, now we have to be careful not to be convicted of the crime of 'transphobia.'

In the area of sexuality, Christians under the authority of the Bible run completely contrary to the attitudes and actions promulgated and promoted by the world. The world has no absolutes in this area. It preaches total licence. Although even the world would baulk at paedophilia, two or more consenting adults are free almost to indulge in whatever they like.

Back to the Bible

Christians however are not free to do what they like. It is from the Bible, the Word of God, that we take our instructions as to what we are to believe and how we are to behave, sexual attitudes and actions included. God our Maker knows best, and according to the Bible, the will of God confines sexual activity solely within the boundaries of monogamous, heterosexual marriage. In Hebrews 13:4 we read 'Let marriage be held in honour among all, and let the marriage bed be undefiled; for God will judge the immoral and adulterous.'

The verse here forbids sexual activity before marriage, viewing it as 'immoral.' Elsewhere Paul writes *'Be sure of this, that no fornicator or impure man ... has any inheritance in the kingdom of Christ and of God'* (Ephesians 5:5). Habitual fornicators, who blatantly flout God's law, reveal that they have never been born again, and are thus currently heading for hell, and will spend eternity there unless they repent and turn to God in Christ for mercy.

The verse here in Hebrews 13:4 also forbids those who are married from engaging and indulging in sexual activity outside of the marriage bond, designating such as adultery. Hence the will of God confines sexual activity to marriage and enjoins sexual abstinence and purity on those who are single.

God's confining of sexual activity solely within the marriage bond is to help and not hinder us. God's commandments are His enablements. You can be sure that He does not give us a commandment which we are unable to keep. He gives us sufficient grace to do His will. God's commandments are given for our safety and well being. The family is the basic building block of society. Fornication and adultery weaken and break up this basic building block. Marriage gives a safe and stable environment for the nurture of children. When children suffer – as they do when a family is broken up due to adultery – the whole society suffers.

In believing and teaching the above, Christians are accused of 'not moving with the times.' God's moral law however is timeless – applicable to all societies at all times. God's law is the Maker's own instruction for a happy life. His law keeps us from harm, and God's seventh commandment in Exodus 20:14 is clear *'You shall not commit adultery.'* Proverbs 6:32-33 warns *'He who commits adultery has no sense; he who does it destroys himself. Wounds and dishonour will he get, and his disgrace will not be wiped away.'*

The *Heidelberg Catechism* elucidates the seventh commandment in this way:

Q. What does the seventh commandment teach us?

A. That all unchastity is accursed of God; and that we should therefore loath it from the heart, and live chastely and modestly whether in holy wedlock or single life.

Q. Does God in this commandment forbid nothing more than adultery and such like gross sins?

Q. Since our body and soul are both temples of the Holy Ghost, it is His will that we keep both pure and holy; for which reason He forbids all unchaste actions, gestures, words, thoughts, desires and whatever may entice thereunto.

Christian marriage

According to the Bible therefore, sexual activity is to be confined solely within a committed, monogamous, heterosexual, life-long marriage relationship. This is the norm for everyone, whether Christian or non-Christian – though a Christian is free to be married *'only in the Lord'* (1 Corinthians 7:39), that is, only to a fellow believer. Should a Christian marry a non Christian they will have unshared treasure and many difficulties detrimental to the Christian's faith. A 'mixed marriage' is described in the Bible as an 'unequal yoke.' The term is taken from eastern agriculture. When a yoke is unequal, the two partners are not pulling and working together. Should a Christian marry a non Christian, the different priorities of the two parties will cause difficulties and tensions, and the Christian will come off worse. The prohibition of a mixed marriage actually goes back BC. It was seen as spiritually hazardous even in Old Testament times. When God's people entered Canaan, God stipulated *'You shall not make marriages with them, giving your daughters to their sons or taking their daughters for your sons, for they would turn away your sons from following Me to serve other gods ...'* (Deuteronomy 7:3-4).

Marriage made in heaven

Monogamous, heterosexual marriage – the only safe arena for sexual activity – is not man's idea but God's. It actually originated in the Garden of Eden. It is thus a creation ordinance. God Himself performed the first marriage ceremony when, after creating Eve out of the side of Adam, He brought her to Adam (Genesis 2:22). Scripture then enunciates a principle which is and will be valid as long as this world lasts when it says *'Therefore a man leaves his father and his mother and cleaves to his wife, and they become one flesh'* (Genesis 2:24). This was endorsed by the Lord Jesus Christ Himself when He said *'Have you not read that He who made them from the beginning made them male and female'*, and said *'For this reason a man shall leave his father and mother and be joined to his wife, and the two shall become one flesh. So they are no longer two but one flesh.' What therefore God has joined together, let no man put asunder'* (Matthew 19:4-6).

The Saviour here is echoing the sentiment of Genesis 1:27, where we read *'So God created man in His own image, in the image of God He created him; male and female He created them.'* Underscore those words *'male and female He created them.'* The Bible teaches the complementarity of the gender. The Bible teaches that the gender are distinct. The

Bible teaches that men and women complement and 'fit' each other, physically and emotionally. Genesis 1:27 teaches that there are only two sexes: male and female and they are complementary. It is this which makes the current day promotion of homosexuality and transexuality contrary to the will of God. It is here especially that Christians live in a Christian counter culture, against the grain of the current climate.

Homosexuality

The Bible prohibits homosexuality. Why? Because it is contrary to the male/female created order. It is contrary to the way God has ordained the continuation of the human race. To be blunt, two men or two women cannot produce a baby! Homosexuality is condemned by God. *'You shall not lie with a male as with a woman; it is an abomination'* (Leviticus 18:22).

Genesis 19:24 describes how God *'rained on Sodom and Gomorrah brimstone and fire'* due to their indulgence in homosexuality. We get the word 'sodomy' from this incident. The incident is recorded for posterity as a real-life warning. 'Just as Sodom and Gomorrah and the surrounding cities, which acted immorally and indulged in unnatural lust, serve as an example by undergoing a punishment of eternal fire' (Jude 7). 'Unnatural lust'? Yes, for homosexuality goes against the natural order created and ordained by God.

Likewise, it is the distinction which demarks the two sexes which also prohibits transexuality. Gender is biologically determined. It is genetic. Why? Because 'Male and female He created them' – with either X or Y chromosomes. God has His distinct roles for males and females. (Men cannot conceive children, and women cannot sire children). Male and female are distinct. Hence Deuteronomy 22:5 *'A woman shall not wear anything that pertains to a man, nor shall a man put on a woman's garment; for whoever does these things is an abomination to the LORD our God.'*

Homosexuality and transexuality are thus both contrary to the will of God. They are literally and metaphorically 'against the grain.' They cannot be countenanced if we claim to believe that the Bible is the Word of God and contains the secret of a happy life, a happy death and a happy eternity. Whilst there are ordained 'Christian' ministers who are openly 'gay', a 'gay Christian' is as contradictory as sweet salt, savoury sugar or a square circle.

The grace of God

Does all the above which has been written seem harsh on an increasingly large segment of society? It would be if it were not for the grace of God. God's grace will enable us to live a happy, contended and pure single life, if singleness is His will for us. God's grace will also enable us to be faithful in marriage and even to increase in love for our spouse as the years go by, and never think about lusting for anyone else. God's saving grace can even reach an out and out homosexual. Through Christ, their sin may be forgiven, just as through Christ all sin can be forgiven. And by God's Holy Spirit, homosexuals and those guilty of any sexual sin, may know self control and overcome their lust and a gradual weakening of those tendencies which God condemns. God's grace is a transforming grace. 2 Corinthians 5:17 reads *'Therefore, if any one is in Christ, he is a new creation, the old has passed away, behold the new has come.'*

Did you know that the Christian congregation at Corinth contained former homosexuals along with others guilty of sexual sin. Corinth was notorious for such people. Former though is the operative word, because they had been saved out of that life by the grace of God in Christ. Paul reminded them of this in a letter he wrote to the church in vice-filled Corinth:

'Do you not know that the unrighteous will not inherit the kingdom of God? Do not be deceived; neither the immoral, nor idolaters, nor adulterers, nor sexual perverts ... will inherit the kingdom of God. <u>And such were some of you.</u> But you were washed, you were sanctified, you were justified in the name of the Lord Jesus Christ and in the Spirit of our God' (1 Corinthians 6:9-11).

Christians therefore practice sexual purity. Anything else is foolish. Anything else suggests we know better than Almighty God. Anything else will reap what it sows, perhaps in this life, but certainly in the life to come. *'Do not be deceived; God is not mocked, for whatever a man sows, that he will also reap'* (Galatians 6:7).

CHAPTER TEN

A Christian Abstains from Artificial Stimulants

Alcohol and drugs may be described as 'beloved enemies.' They give temporary pleasure and 'highs', but then bring wrecked lives in their wake. Alcohol and drugs though are very much part of the 'scene' in our 21st century society.

Prescribed drugs, when taken medicinally and under medical care can be beneficial. Perhaps we should 'say grace' before taking them! God uses 'means' for our blessing. Medicine is one of His 'means.' Illegal drugs however, for example, cannabis, cocaine, amphetamines et al are another matter. Many have got 'hooked' on the temporary sensation such drugs give. Likewise with alcohol. The latter is supposedly needed for a 'good time' or to blot out sorrows and escape from reality. Drugs and alcohol take a hold on people, and lead to much misery and poverty. Addiction to drugs and drink is a societal problem which the authorities cannot solve. Then many, whilst not having an addiction, would yet secretly admit that they have difficulties in this area. It controls them, rather than them controlling it.

Whilst both alcohol and drugs are an accepted part of certain segments and circles of society, this is not the case in Christian circles. A Christian will abstain from all artificial stimulants. A Christian will actually have no need for artificial stimulations, for God will most certainly give us grace to avoid both them and the harm they bring. Why though does a Christian abstain from taking artificial stimulants?

1. Because our bodies matter

In 1 Corinthians 6:19 Paul writes *'Do you not know that your body is a temple of the Holy Spirit within you, which you have from God? ...'* In Old Testament times, God manifested His visible presence in the tabernacle and temple. Then in the fullness of time, God presenced Himself in a human body – He became incarnate in the Lord Jesus Christ. *'In Him the whole fullness of deity dwells bodily'* (Colossians 2:9). The wonder of wonders is that now, Almighty God actually inhabits Christians! He condescends to dwell in us by His Holy Spirit. 'Your body is a temple of the Holy Spirit within you.' It is this which makes the Christian's body sacred. It is for this reason that we should take care of our bodies, and not abuse them with drink, drugs or anything else. We cannot do what we like with our bodies, as they are the dwelling place of God's Holy Spirit. Our bodies are not our own. They belong to God – they have been redeemed and will yet be fully redeemed by Christ, and are to be used as a vehicle for His glory. *'Do you not know that your body is a temple of the Holy Spirit within you, which you have from God? You are not your own; you were bought with a price. So glorify God in your body'* (1 Corinthians 6:19-20).

2. Because God gives grace

Alcohol and drugs are many peoples' 'coping mechanism.' They need them as a crutch to get through life. Who can deny that life has many difficulties, stresses, strains, storms and sorrows? We live in a fallen world. Misery is a consequence of sin. How do we cope with living in such conditions? A Christian does not turn to a bottle. Rather, a

Christian turns to the Lord. We have a loving Father in heaven. We have a sympathetic Saviour who knows all about the sorrows of this world. We are promised the help of God's Holy Spirit, the divine comforter – the 'parakletos', the 'one called alongside to help.'
On one occasion when the Apostle Paul was really 'going through it', God promised him *'My grace is sufficient for you'* (2 Corinthians 12:9). Every Christian, whatever their need, can lay claim to this promise. Almighty God will give us the strength and ability to live within the boundaries of the circumstances He has ordained for us. *'As your days, so shall your strength be'* (Deuteronomy 33:25). *'No temptation has overtaken you that is not common to man. God is faithful, and He will not let you be tempted beyond your strength, but with the temptation will also provide the way of escape, that you may be able to endure it'* (1 Corinthians 10:13). *'He gives more grace'* (James 4:6).

> He giveth more grace when the burdens grow greater
> He sendeth more strength when the labours increase
> To added affliction He addeth His mercy
> To multiplied trials, His multiplied peace
>
> When we have exhausted our store of endurance
> When our strength has failed ere the day is half done
> When we reach the end of our hoarded resources
> Our Father's full giving is only begun
>
> His love has no limit, His grace has no measure
> His power has no boundary known unto man
> For out of His infinite riches in Jesus
> He giveth, and giveth and giveth again.

3. Because Christians know true and lasting joy

Truth be told, Christians have no need of any artificial stimulants to induce a temporary high, as we are already intoxicated! We are intoxicated by the love and grace of God. Christian salvation – knowing Christ and His benefits – is a source of lasting joy which this world can neither give nor take away.

> Saviour, since of Zion's city
> I through grace a member am
> Let the world deride or pity
> I will glory in Thy Name
> Fading is the worldling's pleasure
> All his boasted pomp and show
> Solid joys and lasting treasure
> None but Zion's children know.

In Nehemiah 8:10 we read *'The joy of the LORD is your strength.'* Strange as it may sound, God actually commands His people to be joyful – and if we belong to His people, we have every reason to be joyful. In Philippians 4:4 Paul exhorts 'Rejoice in the Lord always; again I will say rejoice.' The joy of the Christian then is a specific joy. It is a joy distinctly 'in the Lord':

In the Lord - for He is the absolute ruler, and is governing our lives for our eternal blessing.

In the Lord - for He has adopted us into His family, and so we may know and address God as 'Abba, Father.'

In the Lord - for we are the objects of His saving grace.

In the Lord - for He has promised us His all-sufficient sustaining grace.

In the Lord – for our chief end is 'to glorify God and to enjoy Him for ever.' (*Shorter Catechism*).

In the Lord – for He will never fail us or forsake us. *'The LORD is my Shepherd, I shall not want'* (Psalm 23:1).

In the Lord – for His love is the greatest joy of all and will last for ever when all else is gone.

Knowing Christ and the fullness of His salvation is the antidote to all the negative offerings of this world, such as drink or drugs. Only Christ can satisfy. Once we know the satisfaction and spiritual satiation which only Christ can bring, other sinful and destructive cravings will lose their attraction and power.

> Now none but Christ can satisfy
> None other name for me
> There's love and life and lasting joy
> Lord Jesus found in Thee.

So a Christian abstains and will have nothing to do with the artificial stimulants – drink and drugs – with which the world tempts, entices and allures. Drugs, of course, are illegal. They wreck bodies, families and finances, and lead to poverty and criminality. Alcohol is not illegal. It is widely advertised. Such advertising though masks the misery it causes – road accidents, domestic violence, broken homes, lost jobs … If alcohol was a dog it would be put down! No Christian in their right mind, keen to keep their testimony intact, will drink alcohol today. What about 'moderate drinking'? No. Every alcoholic began as a 'moderate drinker.' Paul writes *'do not get drunk with wine, for that is debauchery, but be filled with the Spirit'* (Ephesians 5:18). Beware of alcohol and give it a wide berth. Heed the ancient writer who wrote: *'Who has woe? Who has sorrow? Who has strife? Who has complaining? Who has wounds without cause? Who has redness of eyes? Those who tarry long over wine, those who go to try mixed wine. Do not look at wine when it is red, when it sparkles in the cup and goes down smoothly. At the last it bites like a serpent, and stings like an adder'* (Proverbs 23:29-32).

CHAPTER ELEVEN

Eternity will finally Distinguish Christians from Non Christians

The difference between a Christian and a non Christian is not always apparent in this life, even if it ought to be. Some Christians, for various reasons, are like Joseph of Arimathea *'who was a disciple of Jesus, but secretly, for fear of the Jews'* (John 20:38). To his credit however, Joseph did not remain a secret disciple, but came out into the open, going boldly to Pontius Pilate to ask for the body of Jesus, so that he could give Him a dignified burial.

All will be revealed

If the difference between a Christian and a non Christian is not always distinct in this life, we can say with certainty that it assuredly will be in the life to come – fully, finally and forever. And the difference could not be more stark or greater. John 3:36 states *'He who believes in the Son has eternal life; he who does not obey the Son shall not see life but the wrath of God rests upon him.'* Similarly, in 1 John 5:11-12 we read *'And this is the testimony, that God gave us eternal life, and this life is in His Son. He who has the Son has life; he who has not the Son of God has not life.'*

Non-Christians are described in the Bible as *'having no hope and without God in the world'* (Ephesians 2:12). Christians however have the *'hope* (that is, confident expectation) *of eternal life which God who never lies promised ages ago, and at the proper time manifested in His Word'* (Titus 1:2-3).

Endless hope

According to the Bible, Christians have and will have endless hope, while those without Christ, sadly, will come to a hopeless end. By means of Christ's reconciliatory work on the cross, a Christian enjoys fellowship with God, and a Christian will yet enjoy fellowship with God for all eternity. The salvation which Christ wrought will be enjoyed by the Christian hereafter as well as here – in the life to come as well as in the present life. Indeed, the fellowship with God which Christians enjoy will be enjoyed in a much fuller, richer way in the life to come, unhindered and un-handicapped by all which impedes our fellowship with Him in the present age. Psalm 16:11 reads *'Thou dost show me the path of life; in Thy presence there is fullness of joy, in Thy right hand are pleasures for evermore.'*

Paul could say – along with every believer – that *'For to me to live is Christ and to die is gain'* (Philippians 1:21). And notwithstanding life's present joys, both can also say *'My desire is to be with Christ, for that is far better'* (Philippians 1:23). For the Christian, the best is yet to be, for *'What no eye has seen, nor ear heard, nor the heart of man conceived, what God has prepared for those who love Him'* (1 Corinthians 2:9).

The resurrection of the body

The Christian's ultimate prospect is not actually the salvation of the soul but the resurrection of the body – living in glorious bodies on a redeemed earth, able to love and serve God in a way that was up until then unknown. The guarantee of this is Christ's own resurrection. The guarantee of this is that we belong to Christ. *'Christ has been raised from the dead, the first fruits of those who have fallen asleep. For as by a man came death, by a man has come also the resurrection of the dead. For as in Adam all die, so also in Christ shall all be made alive'* (1 Corinthians 15:20-22). Christians shall yet be raised to a glorious immortality! The *Apostles' Creed* fittingly concludes with 'I believe in ... the resurrection of the body and the life everlasting. Amen.'

The *Heidelberg Catechism* elucidates what we are talking about further when it explains in its question-and-answer form:

Q. What comfort does the resurrection of the body afford you?
A. That not only my soul, after this life, shall be immediately taken up to Christ its Head; but also this body, raised by the power of Christ, shall again be united with my soul, and made like unto the glorious body of Christ.

Q. What comfort have you from the article of the 'life everlasting'?
A. That, inasmuch as I now feel in my heart the beginning of eternal joy, I shall after this life possess complete bliss, such as eye has not seen, nor ear heard, neither entered into the heart of man; therein to praise God for ever.

Q. But what does it help you now that you believe all this?
A. That I am righteous in Christ before God, and an heir of eternal life.

Q. How are you righteous before God?
A. Only by true faith in Jesus Christ ...

So the Christian's prospects are glorious. By His saving grace in Christ, we will yet 'glorify God and enjoy Him for ever.' All will be well. Nothing will be able to sever us from His love.

The non-Christian's 'prospects'

In complete, infinite and eternal contrast to the Christian, the non Christian's future – according to Scripture – could not be bleaker. A non-Christian has no Saviour, and thus will be held accountable for their own sins. God has to punish sin, as His justice is part of His very God-ness. Sin has to be punished either in the sinner or in a substitute for the sinner. Believers know and rejoice in Christ as their Saviour-substitute – their 'propitiation'; the One who turns aside the wrath of God due to them. Non believers however do not. Thus *'the wrath of God rests upon them'* (John 3:36). Formidably then, at the end of the age, eternal punishment will be the lot of those outside of Christ. Most terrifyingly, Scripture foretells of the divine *'vengeance upon those who do not know God and upon those who do not obey the gospel of our Lord Jesus. They shall suffer the punishment of eternal destruction and exclusion from the presence of the Lord and from the glory of His might'* (2 Thessalonians 1:8-9).

And so we see the eternal difference between the Christian and the non Christian which is yet to be made manifest. It is the difference between heaven and hell. It is the difference between blessing and burning. It is the difference between knowing the eternal pardon of God or the eternal punishment of God – justification or condemnation. The Bible reveals the eternal blessedness of the believer and the eternal punishment of those outside of Christ and the saving grace of God. It is this which gives the gospel – the message of salvation – its urgency. *'Believe in the Lord Jesus and you will be saved'* (Acts 16:31). *'Behold, now is the acceptable time; behold, now is the day of salvation'* (2 Corinthians 6:2). *'How shall we escape if we neglect such a great salvation'* (Hebrews 2:3).

Where will you spend eternity?

It is saving faith in the Lord Jesus Christ – or the lack of it – which determines whether we spend eternity eternally saved or eternally lost. A distinction of the Christian Faith is its urgent evangelistic thrust: How imperative it is that we avail ourselves of Christ's saving work while we may.

> Where will you spend eternity?
> This question comes to you and me
> Tell me, what shall your answer be
> Where will you spend eternity?
>
> Many are choosing Christ today
> Turning from all their sins away
> Heaven shall their happy portion be
> Where will you spend eternity?
>
> Leaving the strait and narrow way
> Going the downward road today
> Sad will the final ending be
> Lost through a long eternity!
>
> Repent, believe this very hour
> Trust in the Saviour's grace and power
> Then shall your joyous answer be
> Saved through a long eternity.

Soli Deo Gloria

Inspired to write a book?

Contact

Maurice Wylie Media
Inspirational Christian Publisher

Based in Northern Ireland and distributing around the world.

www.MauriceWylieMedia.com

To contact the author visit
www.TimothyJCross.org

www.ingramcontent.com/pod-product-compliance
Lightning Source LLC
Chambersburg PA
CBHW071540080526
44588CB00011B/1738